THE BOOK OF
THE BOOK

Books by Idries Shah

Sufi Studies and Middle Eastern Literature
The Sufis
Caravan of Dreams
The Way of the Sufi
Tales of the Dervishes: *Teaching-stories Over a Thousand Years*
Sufi Thought and Action

**Traditional Psychology,
Teaching Encounters and Narratives**
Thinkers of the East: *Studies in Experientialism*
Wisdom of the Idiots
The Dermis Probe
Learning How to Learn: *Psychology and Spirituality in the Sufi Way*
Knowing How to Know
The Magic Monastery: *Analogical and Action Philosophy*
Seeker After Truth
Observations
Evenings with Idries Shah
The Commanding Self

University Lectures
A Perfumed Scorpion (Institute for the Study of Human Knowledge and California University)
Special Problems in the Study of Sufi Ideas (Sussex University)
The Elephant in the Dark: *Christianity, Islam and the Sufis* (Geneva University)
Neglected Aspects of Sufi Study: *Beginning to Begin* (The New School for Social Research)
Letters and Lectures of Idries Shah

Current and Traditional Ideas
Reflections
The Book of the Book
A Veiled Gazelle: *Seeing How to See*
Special Illumination: *The Sufi Use of Humour*

The Mulla Nasrudin Corpus
The Pleasantries of the Incredible Mulla Nasrudin
The Subtleties of the Inimitable Mulla Nasrudin
The Exploits of the Incomparable Mulla Nasrudin
The World of Nasrudin

Travel and Exploration
Destination Mecca

Studies in Minority Beliefs
The Secret Lore of Magic
Oriental Magic

Selected Folktales and Their Background
World Tales

A Novel
Kara Kush

Sociological Works
Darkest England
The Natives Are Restless
The Englishman's Handbook

Translated by Idries Shah
The Hundred Tales of Wisdom (Aflaki's *Munaqib*)

THE BOOK OF THE BOOK

Idries Shah

The value of the dwelling
is in the dweller.
Saying

ISF PUBLISHING

Contents

Preface

A LIONESS, ACCORDING to Aesop, was asked by some other animals how many cubs she produced at one birth.
  She said:

'One – but that one is a lion.'

Idries Shah

1

The Dervish Who Became a King

There was once a dervish who had seen Truth.

He decided that he would have to become
powerful in the ordinary world before people
would listen to him, so he applied all his
concentration to the task of attaining visible
authority.

In the course of time he became a king.

When he had spent some time as a ruler, the
dervish realised that people did not want his
way of teaching.

They appeared to hear him, but acted only from
hope of reward or fear of punishment.

This dervish-king lacked an instrument with
which to teach.

None came to him until he was almost at the end
of his days.

2

The Stranger Dressed in Green

One day the ageing king, out on a hunting
   expedition, had sat down to rest when a
   stranger, dressed in green, approached.
Saluting the king he told him a story, this story,
   The Tale of the Book.
The next Section begins the Tale of the Book.

3

Contrary to Expectation

A wise man, the wonder of his age, taught his
disciples from a seemingly inexhaustible store of
wisdom.

He attributed all his knowledge to a thick tome
which was kept in a place of honour in his
room.

The sage would allow nobody to open the volume.

When he died, those who had surrounded him,
regarding themselves as his heirs, ran to open
the book, anxious to possess what it contained.

They were surprised, confused and disappointed
when they found that there was writing on only
one page.

They became even more bewildered and then
annoyed when they tried to penetrate the
meaning of the phrase which met their eyes.

It was: 'When you realise the difference between
the container and the content, you will have
knowledge.'

4

The Opinion of the Scholars

The successors to the sage took the book to the
   most famous scholars of the times, saying:
'We have this book, and seek your interpretation.
It belonged to such-and-such a sage, the wonder of
   the age, now dead.
This is all he left behind, and we are unable to
   fathom its mystery.'
At first the scholars were delighted to see a work
   of such size, bearing the name of its former
   owner, whom they knew to have been revered
   by multitudes of people.
They said:
'We will of course give you the real interpretation.'
But when they found that the book was all but
   empty, and what words there were made no
   sense to them, they first sneered and then
   shouted at the students, driving them away in
   their fury.
They believed that they had been victims of a
   hoax.
That was a time when scholars were limited and
   literal-minded.
They could not imagine a book which could *do*
   something, only a book which *said* something.

5

The Interpretation of the Dervish

The dispirited students, going to rest in a
    caravanserai, came upon a dervish, and told him
    of their perplexity.
He said:
'What did you learn from the scholars?'
The travellers said:
'Nothing. They could tell us nothing.'
The dervish said:
'On the contrary, they told you everything.
They showed that the book was not to be
    understood in the manner assumed by you, or
    by them.
You may think that they lack depth.
But you, in your turn, lack sense.
The book was teaching something through the
    incident itself, while you remained asleep.'
But the students found this explanation too subtle
    for their minds, and the only person who
    maintained the knowledge of the book was a
    casual visitor to the caravanserai, who overhead
    the interchange which I have just repeated to
    you, O King and Dervish!
The stranger dressed in green then stood up and
    walked away.

6

The Guarding and Theft of the Book

The king was so impressed by the stranger's story
that he ordered the story to be inscribed and
bound in a large book.

This was placed in a niche in his treasury and
guarded by armed men, day and night.

The aged king died and a barbarian conqueror
devastated his realm.

Breaking into the treasury, this man saw the book
in its place of honour and said to himself: 'This
must be the source of the country's happiness,
wisdom and prosperity.'

He said aloud: 'Let the book be taken down and
read out to me in our own language.'

But this conqueror, for all his physical power, was
an ignoramus; he could make no sense from the
words in the book.

7

Mali Saves the Book

The barbarian had the book destroyed, but his
   interpreter, whose name was Mali, remembered
   its contents.
It is through his work that its teaching was passed
   down. Mali opened a shop.
He kept copies of *The Book of the Book* on view,
   for sale.
Nobody was allowed to look inside until he had
   paid two gold pieces for a copy.
Some learned the lesson of the book, and came
   back to study with Mali.
Others wanted their money returned, but Mali
   always said:
'I cannot give you back your money until you
   return me what you have learned from the
   transaction, as well as the book itself.'
Some who preferred mere appearance to inner
   content, called Mali a deceiver.
But Mali told them: 'You were, all along, seeking
   deceivers, so you will assume that you have
   found one in anyone.'

8

Yasavi Buys It for Twelve Gold Pieces

When Ahmed Yasavi was a student, he bought a copy of The Book from Mali, paying two gold pieces.

The following day he returned, and gave Mali another ten pieces of gold, saying: 'What I have learned from The Book is worth more than this.

But since I have no more money I give it all to you, in token of my valuing this lesson as equal to my entire possessions.'

9

Yasavi of the Masters Transmits It

Yasavi had the history and the content of *The
  Book of the Book* bound in a volume of over
  two hundred pages, on whose cover was
  written:
  'If the thickness of books determines the value
  of their content, this one should assuredly be
  even thicker.'
Since Ahmed Yasavi, of the Masters of Central
  Asia, this story has been transmitted for more
  than seven hundred years.

A Request

If you enjoyed this book, please review it on Amazon and Goodreads.

Reviews are an author's best friend.

To stay in touch with news on forthcoming editions of Idries Shah works, please sign up for the mailing list:

     http://bit.ly/ISFlist

And to follow him on social media, please go to any of the following links:

     https://twitter.com/idriesshah

     https://www.facebook.com/IdriesShah

     http://www.youtube.com/idriesshah999

     http://www.pinterest.com/idriesshah/

     http://bit.ly/ISgoodreads

     http://idriesshah.tumblr.com

http://idriesshahfoundation.org

CPSIA information can be obtained
at www.ICGtesting.com
Printed in the USA
BVHW071235271221
624762BV00004B/292